Grand Favorites for Piano

12 Late Intermediate Arrangements of Classical Themes and Folk Songs

Melody Bober

Time-honored classics and cherished folk songs have always been part of my teaching studio for several reasons. Music of all varieties, from spirituals to operas, tell stories. Traditional folk songs give students the opportunity to enjoy the same music that their parents and grandparents loved when they were children. Additionally, learning classical themes introduces students to historically significant repertoire and famous composers.

In the spirit of keeping traditional music alive, I have written *Grand Favorites for Piano*, Book 6. The collection offers students a great learning experience and a means to progress technically and musically.

It is my hope that students find the beloved melodies fun to practice, enjoyable to perform, and appreciated by audiences everywhere!

Best wishes,

CONTENTS

Alfred Music
P.O. Box 10003
Van Nuys, CA 91410-0003
alfred.com

Copyright © 2019 by Alfred Music
All rights reserved. Printed in USA.

ISBN-10: 1-4706-4182-8
ISBN-13: 978-1-4706-4182-5

Cover Image:
Stars (Seamless) © Getty Images / Leontura

Beautiful Dreamer

Stephen Foster (1826–1864)
Arr. Melody Bober

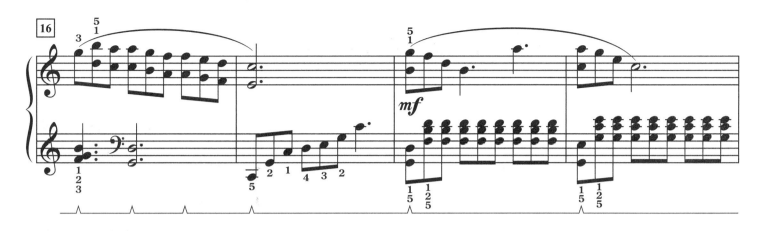

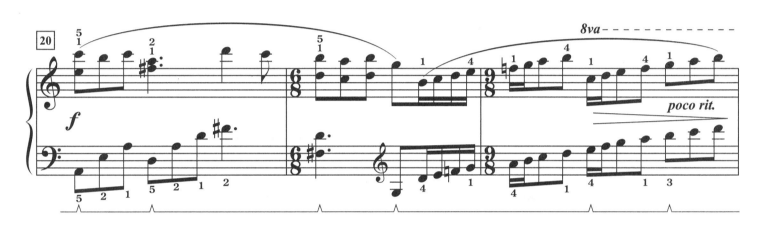

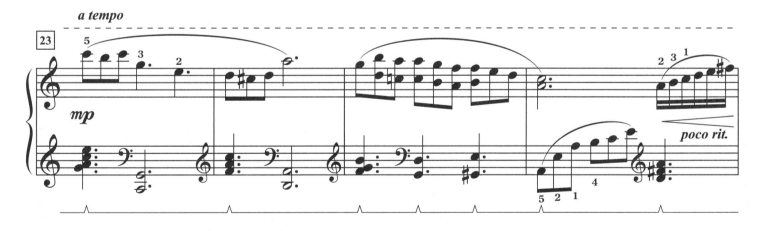

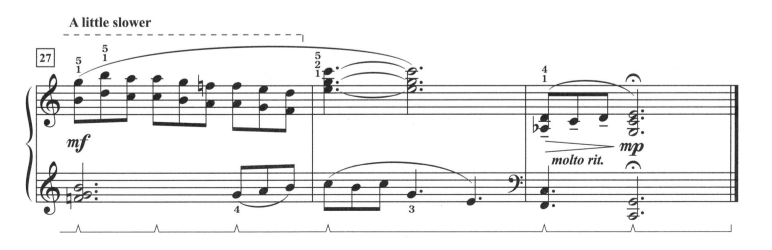

You're a Grand Old Flag

George M. Cohan (1878–1942)
Arr. Melody Bober

Scarborough Fair

Traditional English
Arr. Melody Bober

Choucoune
(Yellow Bird)

Michel Mauléart Monton (1855–1898)
Arr. Melody Bober

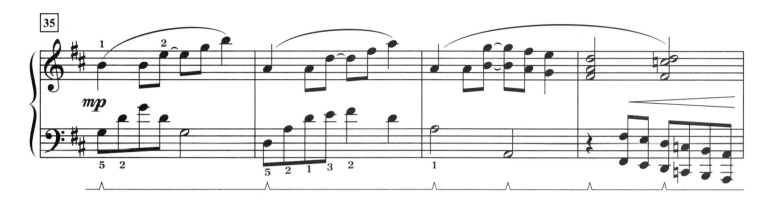

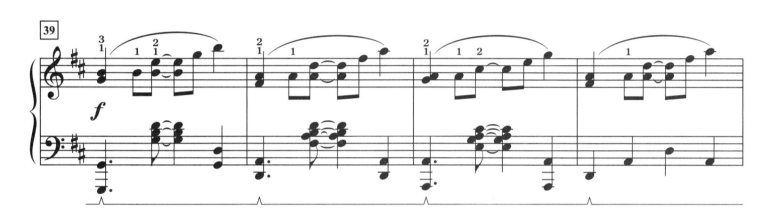

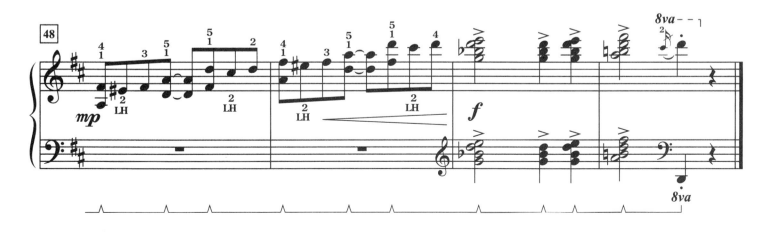

The Yellow Rose of Texas

Traditional
Arr. Melody Bober

Hornpipe

(from the *Water Music* suite)

George Frideric Handel (1685–1759)
Arr. Melody Bober

Greensleeves

Traditional English
Arr. Melody Bober

Minuet
(from *String Quintet in E Major*)

Luigi Boccherini (1743–1805)
Arr. Melody Bober

Blue Danube Waltz

Johann Strauss II (1825–1899)
Arr. Melody Bober

America

(My Country, 'Tis of Thee)

Traditional
Arr. Melody Bober

Hungarian Dance No. 5

Johannes Brahms (1833–1897)
Arr. Melody Bober

Key change

Tempo I

3/28

The Erie Canal

Thomas S. Allen (1876–1919)
Arr. Melody Bober